Lea J. Sorensen

Bear Goes Shopping

Lea J. Sorensen

BEAR GOES SHOPPING

LEA J. SORENSEN

Bear Goes Shopping

Published 2003, 2011, 2025
ISBN: 9780973621310
Library and Archives Canada (891) 997-9565

Lea J. Sorensen

DEDICATION
This book is dedicated to my daughter
Denise.
For the one who has a love of shopping.
May you always continue to enjoy the love of shopping,
regardless if you are just looking, you are being inspired, or
buying the things you need and or want

Bear Goes Shopping

Lea J. Sorensen

Bear Goes Shopping

Bear Goes Shopping

Can you guess what Bear is going to buy?

Lea J. Sorensen

Is Bear going to buy Strawberries or Blueberries?

Bear Goes Shopping

No Bear does not buy Strawberries or Blue berries.
Is Bear going to buy Pasta or Rice?

Lea J. Sorensen

No Bear does not buy Pasta or Rice.
Is Bear going to buy a Lemon or a Lime?

Bear Goes Shopping

No Bear does not buy a Lemon or a Lime.
Is Bear going to buy Plums or Cucumbers?

Lea J. Sorensen

No Bear does not buy Plums or Cucumbers.
Is Bear going to buy Potatoes or an Onion?

Bear Goes Shopping

No Bear does not buy Potatoes or an Onion
Is Bear going to buy an Apple or a Banana?

Lea J. Sorensen

No Bear does not buy an Apple or a Banana.
Is Bear going to buy Cheese or Crackers?

No Bear does not buy Cheese or Crackers.
Is Bear going to buy Peanuts or Oatmeal?

Lea J. Sorensen

No Bear does not buy Peanuts or Oatmeal.
Hmm...Can you guess what Bear is going to buy?

Bear Goes Shopping

Is Bear going to buy Honey?
Yes Bear is going to buy Honey!!
Yumm-Yumm!!

Lea J. Sorensen

Bear Goes Shopping

Author Biography

Lea J. Sorensen is a celebrated children's author known for her captivating stories that spark imagination in young minds. Born in
Calgary, Alberta, and raised in Kamloops, British Columbia, Lea's passion for storytelling was inspired
by her love for teddy bears.

As a Human Service Worker with expertise in supporting high-needs children, youth, and young adults, Lea's experiences have shaped her writing philosophy, which emphasizes imagination, moral lessons, and learning.

With notable works like "Bear in the Mirror" and "Bear Goes Shopping," Lea's books have delighted children and parents alike. Her extensive background in child and youth care, including work in institutions, group homes, foster care, and public education, informs her writing and commitment to creating stories that resonate with young readers.

Lea's dedication to her profession and working with Children, youth, and young adults has earned her recognition and praise for her work in the field of child and youth care and the community, as well as her storytelling.

Her philosophy as an author focuses on crafting stories that inspire, educate, and nurture young minds. With future projects on the horizon, Lea J. Sorensen invites readers to connect with her on social media and join her journey as a children's author."

Follow Lea J. Sorensen on:

Amazon.ca or on Amazon.com,

Bear Goes Shopping

"With my bear collection, Lea J. Sorensen magically bring 'Bear' to life and make him appear to be a real living teddy bear "

About This book:

'Bear' goes to the grocery store and a question by the narrator asks the audience or either by the reader or this book is read to an audience if Bear is going to buy either of the nutritious items in front of Bear. There is a part of the book where the audience guesses what Bear is going to buy allowing the reader or audience to be interactive with the book besides just reading this book.

The Viewer will be:
Shocked!
Surprised!
and eager to continue from one page to the next

This book is full of surprises from the beginning right through to the end!

Other books by this Author/Illustrator
Lea J. Sorensen

A v a i l a b l e B o o k s

Bear In The Mirror Book 1 ISBN: 97809 73621365	Bear Meets Friends: Book 5 ISBN: 9780973621327	Bear Goes Shopping: Book 6 ISBN: 9780973621310
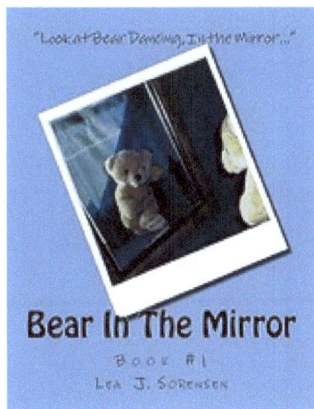		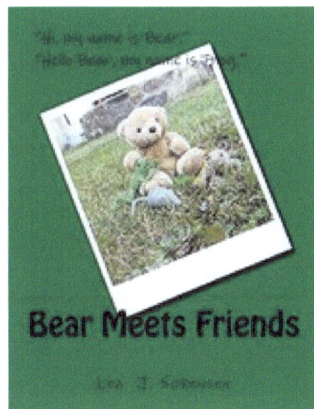

Coming Soon !

-Helping Bear Count 1-10 Book 2
 ISBN: 97809762158

-Bear Goes To The Beach Book 3
 ISBN: 9780973621341

-Bear Does His Warm-Up Exercises,Then His Shapes Book 4
 ISBN: 9780973621334

Bear Goes Shopping

Lea J. Sorensen

Bear Goes Shopping

www.ingramcontent.com/pod-product-compliance
Lightning Source LLC
Chambersburg PA
CBHW041428090426
42741CB00002B/85